THE TIME TO SPEAK IS NOW

DR ANSHUMALI PANDEY

ISBN 979-888591725-4

This Book is dedicated to all the school going Children, and also to those who could not afford better education then they deserved.

Contents

Foreword *vii*

1. Objectives Of Communication 1
2. Meaning Of Communication 6
3. Classification Of Communication 11
4. Speaking Skills 16
5. Using The Telephone 20
6. Listening Skills 23
7. Kinesis & Proximics 29
8. Business Letter 33
9. Barriers Of Communication 39
10. Communication Tips For The Smart Kid On The Block 44

Author 51

Foreword

THE TIME TO SPEAK IS NOW:

Effective Communication is defined as the ability to convey information to another effectively and efficiently. Business managers with good verbal, nonverbal and written communication skills help facilitate the sharing of information between people within a company for its commercial benefit.

However, it is easier said than done.

Communication comes naturally to some, but you must differentiate between a good orator and a good communicator. This book will help you to do exactly that.

Particularly the young children need to start on the right foot of communication and hence I have dedicated the book to them.

Best Wishes..
Dr Anshumali Pandey.

ONE

OBJECTIVES OF COMMUNICATION

OBJECTIVES OF COMMUNICATION:

Every action has an objective or purpose. It may be a reason to attain something though our efforts. Similarly communication at different situations has different objectives which depends on the purpose that has to be achieved. The main objectives of communication are :

1) To inform and provide information to one or to a group is the main objective of communication. The basic of all communication process is transfer of information which can be in any form, verbal or non verbal.

2) To persuade is another important objective. Sometimes customers are needed to be convinced about the quality, price or value for money during product selling process.

3) To motivate staff for high level of productivity is another objective of communication for organizational growth. The bottom line for all organization is profit, and so smooth communication processes are necessary for better performance of the employees.

4) To educate and provide knowledge, the most important means is the medium of communication. Thus through proper communication channels, it can be possible for achieve this objective of educating and spreading knowledge, wherever needed.
5) To train, communication is an integral part designing the courseware and helps in the preparation and delivery of training material so that the trainees can achieve proficiency in specific skills.
6) Communication helps to bring together different units of the group situated at different places under one umbrella, helping in achieving the organizational goal.
7) To relate, building and nurturing mutually beneficial business relationship by keeping in touch with allied persons associated with the organization.
8) Sometimes communication helps us to distress, through entertainment and by social bonding. It is very much required in an organization in developing a healthy working atmosphere where it helps in bringing lighter moments in the work place, thus releasing tension.

Effective communication :

Communication is no communication or not an effective communication if the receiver does not understand what is actually being meant by the sender. The sender may be under the impression that the message has been sent flawlessly, but sometimes it is not so. This is one reason why we see a lot of communication gap between the sender party and the receiver. It is very wrong to just think and feel that the message sent has been understood exactly as it was

meant and there will be perfect execution of the same. Feedback ensures that the message has been received and understood rightly by the receiver exactly the way it was intended by the sender. Thus effective communication takes place only when there is feedback. Miscommunication occurs when there is no confirmation of the message sent.

Communication is effective when it is a two way process. In one way communication, the sender does not come to know whether the message has been understood or not by the receiver. To make the communication effective, the sender should have a well defined objective which creates awareness in the mind of the receiver, thus achieving the goal of communication.

ELEMENTS OR COMPONENTS OF COMMUNICATION :

a) Sender / Speaker / Encoder : The communication process is started by the sender of the message with the main purpose of informing the receiver. All messages are not always spoken, but sometimes written as for letters and emails. Sometimes during SMS, we do not write the full text but use codes as for "u" for "you" or "c" to mean "see". The receiver should be aware of the codes used, thus helping the sender in transmitting a coded message and transfer the information as required.

b) Receiver / Listener / Decoder : The receiver is the target for any message. If the message is spoken, the receiver listens to it, but all messages are not spoken. Whatever may be the way in which the message is transmitted, the receiver gets the message, understands it and tries to perceive the full message as transmitted by the sender, trying to decode the encoded message.

c) Message : The information whether written or spoken which is sent by the sender to the receiver is the message. The message is an organized and structured data, which is formulated in the pre- writing and pre-speaking stage. The data that is delivered by the sender for the understanding of the receiver is a message.

d) Medium : Medium or channel helps the sender to convey the message to the receiver. The different mediums used can be in the form of oral, written or even through gestures and body languages which are referred as non-verbal communication.

e) Feedback : It is the last component of the communication process connecting the receiver to the sender, confirming that the communication has been effective and the message sent has been understood well. Sometimes we nod our head to show our acceptance or move it in different direction to show that we do not accept, or might be speaking it out to second or refuse an idea or may be putting it in writing for confirming our own view on the subject, thus acting as a confirmation to the message sent.

Communication cycle:

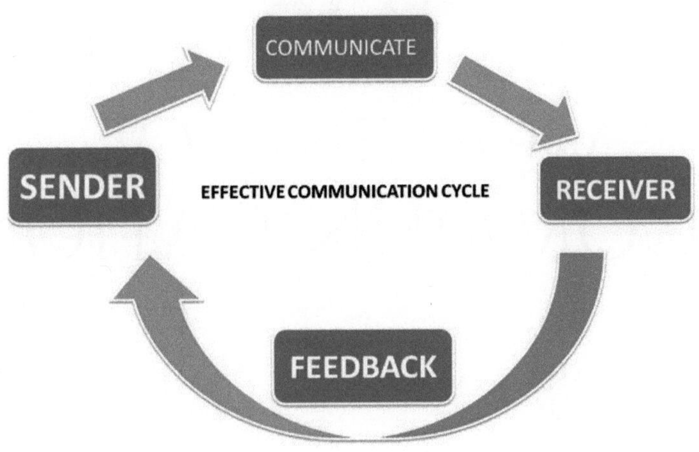
COMMUNICATE
SENDER
EFFECTIVE COMMUNICATION CYCLE
RECEIVER
FEEDBACK

TWO

MEANING OF COMMUNICATION

DEFINITION :

Communication can be defined as the transfer of information from one person to another person or a group at the same level or at different levels.

MEANING OF COMMUNICATION:

Sometimes it is wrongly understood that communication means good English speaking skill. It is not so in the right sense as there are lots of developed countries where English is not widely spoken. Countries like Germany, Japan, etc do not have English as their official language. The scenario is a bit different in India, where English has gained in popularity than other regional languages, and is also been used in official documentation. Although English is more of an urban language in India, the people still uses Hindi or there state vernacular language in many official documentation, thus proving that just knowing English does not mean that a person is sound in communication. Good communication rather refers to a process in which the people expressing his / her views explain it clearly to the person or the group for whom the information was meant.

The world has seen a lot of orators in the form of politicians, corporate stalwarts, media personnel, etc who are excellent in their communication skills. It is by their extreme capability that they address large groups and have great convincing power to establish their point. It is not just the language or the vocabulary that a makes a person good in communication, but it is a combination of lot of factors to ensure a good communication.

ORGANIZATIONAL IMPORTANCE OF COMMUNICATION :

Communication has been one of the most important factors for success in all organizations. All organizations have their vision, mission and goals which should be understood clearly by all associated with the organization. To ensure that all employees understand their personal responsibilities and can be productive in their performance, it is essential to make sure that the top level management passes on the information as directions to their subordinates. If there is any gap in this process, there is likely to be misunderstanding which will result in low level of performance by the staff.

We sometimes have a very vague understanding about the job responsibilities of a manager. Sometimes we see the superficial aspect feeling that it is a very easy task, a comfortable one with no physical tension involved. Whatever be the industry, all managers have one job in common, that is of a good communicator. The manager is a bridge between the management and the staff. The manager attends the meetings to understand the company goals and then releases the same to the subordinate for performance. If a manager wrongly understands the message of the apex management, or fails to make his subordinates understand what the management wants, the result would be very negative in terms of productivity.

Thus the effectiveness of the management completely depends upon the effectiveness of communication. As a manager it is important to ensure that all staff is well aware of every detail that is necessary for their performance. Communication also helps to keep the members informed about the internal and external happenings of the company, which are relevant and of interest to the organization. It is for this reason there are briefings where points are discussed and communicated. Organizations can employ different means of communication. A staff notice board is one of the most common and easy means of communicating with all staff. Thus a proper communication system acts like the nervous system of an organization.

Sometimes communication becomes very essential in all the sub units of a company. This age is referred to as the age of communication where there has been a global development in the field of communication devices. Today mobile phones have replaced telephones, emails have replaced postal services. Life has become much faster. With the development of technology, the entire communication process has speeded. Organizations have accepted the benefits of this development and adopted these techniques to be at pace with the modern world.

A manager is the captain of his team. A leader's success or failure depends on how well he has communicated his plans, visions and ideas to the employees. A manager not only deals with machines but also with humans as employees, clients, guests, subordinates, etc. It is thus one of the most important quality that a manager should posses is his communication skills. This is one sharpest arm that he possesses to motivate, convince and execute his plans in the form of action. It is thus a requirement of all managers to have excellent communication skills for successful functioning of his department.

RELATION BETWEEN COMMUNICATION AND HUMAN RESOURCE :

Communication plays an important role which the management uses to motivate and inspire employees for better productivity. There may be dark phases in our lives, which results in low performance levels. A manager though his experience, delivers motivational and inspirational ideas to boost up the morale of the employees, resulting in greater productivity and success story of the employees.

Communication also plays a vital role in the Training and Development programmes. Guidance is a requisite of all to achieve a peak of perfection. The programmes with improved tools gives better understanding, thus greater impact in the minds. The LCD projectors help us to use audio visual aids where a trainee can use their maximum senses to grasp the topic and use the same in their work place.

Communication also explains disciplinary rules and regulations of the organization. Through the Rule Book, it ensures that all are aware of the rules and regulations that all must adhere to. It clearly mentions about the implementation and the consequences if not followed accordingly.

Communication also helps in maintaining a strong work culture and an excellent working condition. In the present stage it is very much a necessity for the HR department to ensure a healthy working atmosphere. In modern times where both genders work equally at the work place, it is very essential to ensure that all have a respectable atmosphere or else it will lead to heavy staff turnover. The HR department is always working in co-ordination with the operational departments in maintaining such an environment. It is seen that when an employee is happy in his work place, the net result is better productivity. So it is rightly said that motivation, inspiration and a healthy atmosphere all leads to profitability of an organization.

THREE

CLASSIFICATION OF COMMUNICATION

CLASSIFICATION OF COMMUNICATION:

(1) Organizational structure:
(A) Formal (B) Informal

(2) Directional:
(A) Upward (B) Downward (C) Lateral (D) Inward (E) Outward (F)Diagonal

(3) Expressional:
(A) Written (B) Oral (C) Non-verbal (D) Appearance

(1) ORGANIZATIONAL STRUCTURE:

a) Formal:-This kind of communication is formally controlled by managers, which flows through formals channels and is officially recognized. It helps in maintaining the authority structure of the organization and becomes easier to fix responsibility of sub-ordinates in formal communication all information is passed through proper channel which are reliable for compliance act a later stage and avoid distortion of information. Thus formal communication helps to maintain and respect the protocol of the organizational structure.

b) Informal:-It is not officially recognized and sometimes even-dish courage. It exists whenever people get together in groups. It comes from the most intense desire to communicate, share once feeling and thoughts or go sheep. It is also referred to as grape vine because it runs horizontal, vertical and diagonal direction, similar to a vineyard. The advantage of information is a very fast speed. The top management usage this type of communication for feed backs from employs regarding policies, decisions etc to known the reaction of the employs of the organization. There is complete lack of accountability in this kind of communication.

(2) DIRECTIONAL:

a) Upward communication:- It flows from bottom to top which is from a lower position level to a higher level. The main function of upward communication is to supply information to the upward levels. Upward communication includes reports, suggestion, complains etc.

b) Downward communication:-The communication that flows from top to bottom is known as downward communication. This kind of communication exists specially in organization which has an authoritarian atmosphere. Vertical communication can be either written or oral.

<u>Example of written communication:-</u>

1. Instruction
2. Memorandum
3. Letters
4. Hand books

5. Policy and statement
6. Electronics display

Example of oral communication:-

1. Instruction
2. Speeches & announcement
3. Meeting
4. Telephone
5. Loudspeaker

c) Lateral: - When communication takes place between two or more persons who are subordinates working under the same or those who are working at the same level, it is called lateral or horizontal communication. During the course of information view of each other are made known and there is no superior sub~ ordinate relationship.

d) Diagonal or crosswise communication:- It is the flow of information among persons at different levels. Who have ho direct relationship .This is used to speak up the information, improve understanding and coordinates efforts for the achievement of organizational goal.

e) In ward communication: - Communication may be internal or external. Internal communication includes communication within the organization which may be horizontal, vertical or diagonal. In word communication includes are the information receive by the organization form external agencies, which may be other organizations government offices, suppliers, customers share holders, media etc. they may be in the forms of letters, e-mails, word, address, request, suggestion, etc.

f) Outward communication: - It is an ongoing process which allows a company to survive in the competitive world and to written contact and maintains relationship with the people outside. This communication may be oral or written. It may be in the form of advertisement media infractions, public relation, negotiation, mails letters, tenders, telephones, etc.

(3) EXPRESSIONAL:-

(a) Written:- It has come to auger great significance in the lives of individual as well as business organizations. Most business relive on records and written documents rather than on verbal contracts or oral communication.

Function with defined limits of authority and responsibility. Thus a written communication becomes an essential part of any manager's responsibility to communication with the employs with proper documentation. The different method of written communication may include letters, memorandum, notices, minutes, circular, agenda, manuals, handbook, reports, complains, quotations, contracts and forms. The advantage of written communication is that they provide ready references legal deference and they are permanent nature. It facilities to assign responsibilities promotes uniformility in policy and procedure. It also has a few disadvantages like 1st in time consuming, needs expertise, in expression costly and like immediately feedback.

(b) Oral communication: - It is another type of verbal communication which is essentially conversation in nature and has a social purpose. The origin of "grape wine" which is communication in all directions, sharing all shots (all kind) of ideas and feeling lies here. Oral communication can be formal and informal. Formal oral communication takes place during presentations meeting; speech, group discussion and interviews oral communications are two way processes in the presence of receiver and sender. Once deliver can't be erase or mended. It can be carried out between individuals or groups depending on the situation. There is a lot of effective of body language and speech modulation during this process of communication.

Oral communication is very effective during problems receiving. The employees can be influenced and persuaded in the work place to active organizational goals. It gives ready feedback and is time saving and economical. Its disadvantages are there is no documentation and has no legal validity. There is possibility in the distortion of the message and the possibility of miss-understanding.

(c) Non-verbal communication: - It means communication which does not involve speech or words. This is the wordless message receive to the medium to the gesture, sing, body movements, filial expression, tone of voice, etc. Humans convey their feeling by smiling, founding or using wordiness clew. It is instinctive as it indicates the attitude the feeling of the speaker. A non-verbal expression or gesture compliments a verbal message and emphasize or substitute or verbal message.

FOUR
SPEAKING SKILLS

SPEAKING SKILLS:

A speech is a talk given to a large gathering of people especially during occasions like an inauguration, anniversary or any other formal gathering or function. Its purpose is usually to encourage, appreciate, congratulate or to entertain the group being addressed. It is very important for a speaker to overcome the initial fear and nervousness. The speaker should be able to keep the audience engrossed in listening to what he wishes to state. Developing presentation skill is an art where most of the training and learning requires greater focus and attention. Executives and administrators need to strengthen their skills in respect to their presentation.

Steps for successful presentation:

The success of a speaker in regard to the delivery of the speech depends upon the effort that has gone into the preparatory stages. Few steps should be followed so that the presentation creates maximum impact in the mind of the listener. These are :

1) The occasion needs to be considered before delivering the speech.

2) Make audience analysis.
3) The speaker should get acquainted with the environment or location.
4) The manner and mode of presentation needs to be judged beforehand.
5) The planning of the presentation is to be made with the help of a script.
6) It is better if visual aids, handouts and feedback forms are prepared and circulated on or before the presentation.
7) It is very important to rehearse the presentation in advance.
8) Personal aspects of the presenter – physical appearance and body language too creates impression during the presentation.
9) It is very important to ensure that the speaker overcomes nervousness and can be free as much as possible so that the acceptance level is increased.
10) Lastly and most importantly, deliver the presentation with utmost confidence.

The various analysis by the speaker :

Audience Analysis : It is most important for any speaker to understand for whom the presentation is meant. An audience is just not a gathering of people but it has a collective identity of its own. The presentation must be in a form and style that suits and interests the audience and the content and tone should also depend on the nature of the audience.

The age, educational background, experience, etc of the audience are also of great importance for the presentation. The speaker should study the audience before and during the presentation for a better understanding of the audience.

Preliminary analysis : This is another kind of analysis done by the speaker before the speech where the speaker

should reach for the audiences characteristic that will affect his
presentation. The size of the audience influences how formal or informal the speech will be. Other preliminary analysis can be age, gender, background, attitude and appearance in relation to the audience.

Analysis during presentation : This is also called a feedback phase where the speaker gets to know how a listener is receiving his words. With this information the speaker can adjust his presentation to improve the communication result. The analysis can be made through facial expressions of the listeners. It can also be understood by smiles, blank stares, movements, sounds or silence. These are all points to be noted by the speaker to ensure that the listeners give maximum attention to the speech or else there is a need of improvisation.

If the audience is asking questions or if they are answering the questions asked, the speaker understands how well the message has been delivered.

Important qualities possessed by a speaker :

It is often seen that some speakers are favoured over others and their speeches are enjoyed more than others. These speakers touch the heart of their audiences as they posses few qualities that make them unique. A speakers popularity depends on these few qualities of the speaker:

Confidence : The primary characteristic of an effective oral reporting is confidence. Preliminary preparation or rehearsing gives the speaker good confidence during the delivery of his presentation. Even grooming of the speaker adds to his confidence level. For effective communication the speaker should analyze the audience to whom he seeks to reach. The speaker should speak and use simple language and talk in a clear tone to project an image of confidence. Sometimes adding volume to the voice also adds to the confidence level which attracts and impacts the audience.

Sincerity : Listeners always appreciates a sincere speaker. The speaker's preliminary preparation of the draft of his presentation shows his sincerity. The speaker should always make effort to project an image of sincerity to succeed.

Thoroughness : The speaker must be thorough about the subject matter of his presentation. The listeners get impressed about a speaker who is thorough and such impression tends to make the message believable.

Friendliness : A friendly speaker has a significant advantage in communication. A friendly behavior builds up a strong bond between the speaker and the listener, thus helping in effective communication.

FIVE

USING THE TELEPHONE

USING THE TELEPHONE – ETTIQUETTES:

This form of electronic communication, is the most useful and universal medium of oral communication from a distance. STD (Subscriber Trunk Dialing) or ISD (International Subscriber Dialing) are used to speak outside the specific local zone and to places outside the country respectively. A caller identity device attached to the telephone can show the number from which the incoming call is being made.

Handling business calls requires awareness of our unconscious action, which often amounts to bad manners or lack of appropriate skills in effective interpersonal communication.

The first few words spoken by us as a caller or receiver is important in establishing the identity and purpose. It is important to begin with your name, company and purpose specially during official conversations to unknown people. It is a must for a receptionist to answer a call within 3(three) rings, after which the call should be answered with an apology.

It is best to greet with the time of the day, then mentioning the name and the company represented.
Common curtseys while answering a call are :

1) To be polite by using "please" and "thank you" while making a request or when you get a thing done.

2) Use of indirect categorical statements which sounds more like a request,

for example "Could I ...", "May I ...."

The secretary or an assistant's job is also very important and they should be very careful in choosing the words specially when the call cannot be connected or transferred. The call should be put off immediately when it is connected without giving any room to the caller that the call is overheard or tapped.

It is not advisable to discuss any confidential matters over the telephone. They can be over heard or tapped. Use of non verbal skills like tone, sweet voice, proper intonation and articulation of words are required. If all these are followed, it is very helpful in maintaining good business relations.

OTHER MEDIA & MODES OF COMMUNICATION

There have been various media and modes of communication. From the primitive telegraph to telex and fax, these were all various means of communication to far reaching places. Although the science was not so developed as in modern times as we have lightning speed communication connecting the entire world in seconds, through our satellite systems, but there were ways and means before to ensure that the message reaches as fast as possible.

Telegraph : It is a government owned network and works by transmitting sounds in Morse code. It can be sent as ordinary and express. It is used for external communication for contacting customers, suppliers, travelling salesman, etc. It gives an impression of urgency to get immediate response.

Telex : It is an abbreviated form of Teleprinter Exchange. It provides instantaneous communication through direct dial teleprinter to teleprinter system operating at all times of the day. It is obtained from the post office with each subscriber having own identification code for connection. It is charged according to the time taken and the distance it is sent.

Fax : The facsimile machine is a device for transmitting copies of printed images over telephone lines. The receiving machine uses its in built printer to produce an exact photocopy of the original page. It permits quick exchange of information and documents between offices. The print out contains the time, date and the fax number of the sender's machine. The sender gets the confirmation print out showing the receivers fax number, date and time of transmission.

SIX
LISTENING SKILLS

LISTENING SKILLS:

God gave us two ears to do one job, ie to listen. One of the most important factor amongst the four communication skills (reading, writing, speaking and listening), the most crucial is that of listening. It is considered that listening is the most important communication skill for the success of the organization and individual. No oral communication can be effective without proper listening on the part of the receiver of the message.

It involves four major operations as follows :

1) Hearing
2) Understanding
3) Retaining
4) Recalling

It is not the simple ability to decode information. It is a two way exchange in which both parties involved must always be receptive to the thoughts, ideas and emotions of the other. Listening is a mental activity and increases only by consciousness and concentration.

FAULTY LISTENING:

There are also situations when listening is not perfect. These are termed as faulty listening and are mainly due to many factors. The different types of faulty listening are :

1) Pseudo listening – This is a situation when the receiver appears to listen but the mind is somewhere else and there is no willingness to listen. This mainly occurs when the listener is not so interested on the subject of the speaker.
2) Selective listening – This happens when the listener listen only those parts of the message which are of a particular interest or immediate relevance.
3) Self centered listening – In this case the listener is so focused about himself that he uses the time to rehearse on the response instead of listening to him.
4) Fill-in listening – This is also a type of selective listening where the listener leaves gaps in the understanding and then makes an effort to fill in the gaps, sometimes using his own understandings which may not be actual. This happens mainly during forced circumstances.
5) Insulated listening – We choose not to listen to messages that make us very uncomfortable. The example of this kind of listening is with children when they are scolded.
6) Defensive listening – This happens when the listener listens with prior judgment in the mind about what might be said, thus focusing on ideas that aren't even there, interpreting comments as personal attacks when they are not intended that way.
7) Reconstruction listening – This is also called assimilation when we take a new message and reconstruct so that it fits in just like a prior message when all speakers talk about a particular point.

BARRIERS OF LISTENING:

In order to improve the listening skills, listeners need to be aware of the major barriers :

1) **Perceptual barriers** : There are different kinds of perceptual barriers which causes hindrance in the listening process. These barriers arise from certain perceptions that are already in the mind of the listener. Some of these barriers are :

a) Frame of reference - Although the speaker may want to convey a particular meaning, it is the listeners individual frame of reference which determines the actual meaning of the message.

b) Experience and expectation – People perceive information according to their experience and expectations that are based on individual's personality and his experience in similar situation.

c) Relationship with the speaker – Relevant in superior subordinate communication where the subordinate is more conscious of how they perceive communication from the superior.

d) Selective perception : People perceive information according to the individual attitudes and beliefs.

2) **Speaker related barrier** : There are even few barriers related to the speaker. Some of them are :

a) Speed of speech of the speaker.

b) Loudness or softness of the voice of the speaker.

c) Distraction due to long or short pause..

d) Speaker's discussion in relation to the understanding level or capacity of the listener.

e) Unfamiliar expressions used by the speaker.

3) **Listener related barriers** : Barriers of listening can also be sourced from the listener. The various situations where the listener is the barrier are :

a) Uninterested listener
b) Rejecting persons – on a psychological issue or may have a general dislike about the speaker.
c) Mental state of listener : When the listener is mentally lost from the situation due to family issues.
d) Rejecting a subject.
e) Avoiding difficult topic.

4) **Environmental distractions** : There are also other barriers which are related to the environment or the place of communication. Although they do not have a direct link in the communication process, but sometimes they affect communication in a great extent. Some of them are :
a) Uncomfortable seats of the listener.
b) Chatting environment.
c) Unfavourable weather.
d) Odd times of presentation.
e) Disturbances and noises from the environment.
f) Poor lighting and ventilation.

5) **General barriers** : Other than those barriers mentioned above, there are also be few barriers that can affect a smooth communication process. The general barriers are :
a) Fake attention – Deceiving appearance.
b) Listening only for facts – Although individual facts are important, one should be clear about overall goals. Facts are interesting but focus should also be on the rest.

GUIDELINES FOR EFFECTIVE LISTENING:

- One should sit alert and look at the speaker with a view to establish your interest in him
- Stop talking and do not interrupt the speaker unnecessarily

- Observe the non verbal clues of speaker, as this will enable you to grasp the message completely
- The effectiveness of listening generally depends on the intensity of the interest taken
- Look the speaker in the eye as far as possible or follow his movements
- Try to summarize what speaker is trying to say
- Take down notes and link what you listen and what you know about the topic.
- Ask relevant question to yourself so that you can keep on track with the ideas presented by the speaker.

LISTENING AND NOTE TAKING:

Listening and Note taking are correlated. Listening is the skill which helps in taking down notes effectively and the important tips to prepare notes efficiently. So while listening observes the following points for effective note taking:-

- Listen to what is being said and not how it is being said.
- Do not try to write down everything.
- Look for the clues (vocal, postural, Visual) which indicate that those points are important.
- Try to restate what is being said in your own words.
- Use abbreviations as much as possible to increase your note taking speed.
- Take down the notes in one liners as much as possible.
- Underline important words or mark asterisks or stars for the important point which you have noted down.
- Write down definitions and the terms which are new but make sure you understand the point which you are noting down.

- Don't try to note down each and every word, it will distract you from effective listening
- Once you are over with the note taking, go through it again immediately to add certain point which you may remember from your effective listening.

SEVEN

KINESIS & PROXIMICS

KINESIS and PROXIMICS:

Kinesis or **Body language**:- Kinesis literally means body movement, where message is communicated by facial expressions, eye movement and gestures. It is a reflection of thoughts and feelings. It is rightly said that we talk with our tongue but we communicate with our facial expressions.

Kinesis or body language includes:

(a) Facial expression
(b) Eye contact
(c) Gesture
(d) Body posture and
(e) Appearance

(a) Facial expressions : Face is the index of the heart. All our feelings are well reflected and we convey so much without speaking a word. The face and eyes are the most significant means of body communication. The feelings that can generally be communicated by our facial expressions are happiness, disgust, sadness, fear, anger, surprise, etc.

(b) Eye contact : It plays an important role in direct face to face communication. During a conversation, we generally look into the eyes and try to understand the meaning and the innocent feelings. It also helps in building the emotional relationship between the listener and the speaker. It also increases the audience's assessment of the speaker as a credible source. It also establishes and monitors feedback.

(c) Gestures : In addition to facial expressions and eye contact, another important element of kinesis is the use of gestures like physical movement of arms, hands, head, etc. which helps one to express thoughts and to emphasize one's speech. They are directly associated with verbal communication and sometimes display the emotional states. Gestures are generally spontaneous with little control over them.

(d) Body Posture : The body position without specific gestures communicates meaning and conveys variety of messages. It is a way to demonstrate interest in another person or even lack of interest. Postures also indicate cheerfulness, affection, fear, nervousness and also to hide emotions sometimes.

(e) Appearance : It includes clothing, hair, cosmetic, etc. It is rightly said that a person is recognized by his "dress" and "address", where dress refers to the style of attire and address refers to the way he / she speaks to others. The appearance speaks a lot about a person's attitude towards work, life, colleagues, friends, etc.

Proxemics or Space language or surroundings : It is the study of how to communicate with the space around us. It is derived from the word proximity which refers to nearness. To make communication effective, we must take all these factors into consideration and put them to the best possible use.

a) Feature – fixed space – refers to immovable property.

b) Semi fixed feature space – Movable furniture and fixtures in the rooms.

c) Personal Space – the space between at different situations.

a. Intimate – 1'6"

b. Personal – upto 4'

c. Social zone – upto 12'

d. Public zone – above 12'

Artifacts - Our surroundings and colour language : Colour also speak a lot about the ambience of our surroundings. Through our sensory perception we derive a lot of meaning regarding colours and designs.

Colours : Different colours are associated with different behavioural patterns, attitudes and cultural background. People tend to choose the right colour for certain significant occasion.

Different colours seem to signify different moods and mean differently to different people. Happy colours which signify joy are pink, yellow, red, purple and green. On the other hand grey are colours that are associated with feelings that are not so bright. And reflect to some extent an unhappy mood.

White is generally associated with purity and peace. Black is all time power colour and is used to denote quality authority. This proves that there is also an existence of colour language in communication.

Paralanguage : It is very close to oral communication but is considered to be non verbal as it does not comprise of words, but without it words do not convey their intended meaning. The word "para" means "like", which is thus a study of how a speaker verbalizes his words or speech. It includes pronunciation, pitch, volume, pause and other vocal qualities.. Verbal communication consists of the content of words whereas paralanguage involves on "how" of a speaker's voice on the way in which he speaks.

Voice : The first signal that tells us about the speaker's gender, background, education and temperament is through the voice of the speaker. This quality is very important in jobs that include use of telephones, announcing, recording, singing, reciting, etc.

<u>The various factors on which the voice depends are :</u>

a) Pitch Variation : It refers to the sharpness or loudness of the voice. A high pitch is an indication of nervousness and tension.

b) Speaking speed : Speed is not fluency but the pace in which the words are delivered for better understanding by the receiver.

c) Pause : Pace or speed is accompanied by pause. A speaker needs to give sufficient gaps in between words so that the delivery of words are clear and are understood clearly by the audience. When a speaker hardly gives a pause, it too refers to nervousness.

d) Non-fluency : The words "uh", "um", "ah", etc that are used as fillers during a conversation refers to non-fluency of speech. Sometimes it also speaks about the confidence of the speaker on that particular subject.

e) Volume variation : It is necessary for us to speak loud enough to be audible but not too loud to make it sound uncomfortable. It should be adjusted according to the audience. Softness and loudness can alter meaning. Softness appears with affection, sadness, intimacy whereas loudness refers to anger, joy, strength, fearlessness, etc.

EIGHT

BUSINESS LETTER

BUSINESS LETTER:

Letters are the most important form of business communication. There are various kinds of letters through which the organization keeps in touch with the world outside which normally comprises of suppliers, customers, government departments, banks, insurance agencies, transporters, job seekers, etc.

There are different kinds of letters, like :

a) Enquiries, orders, complains and responses to these letters.

b) Sales letters, circulars, memo.

c) Job application and resume.

d) Letters of Personnel Department.

e) Letters from the Accounts Department like correspondence with customers, insurance agencies, banks, etc.

f) Letters from the Administrative Department as in public notices, invitations, correspondence with central and state government, etc.

g) Letters to the Press.

Essentials of a good business letter : Business letters to be good and effective, must have certain essentials and should have certain minimum standards. The language, content, style, context, legth, structure, layout, tone and purpose of a letter are some of the characteristics of a letter. A good business letter should have a clear understanding of all the characteristics to make it effective to sustain good business relationship. A good business letter helps in developing better public relations for the organization. There are few requisites or essentials to make a business letter effective.

The following points are the checklist on which every letter may be evaluated.

1) Clarity : The letter must express the message in clear terms and should be clearly stated.

2) Impact : A letter should create necessary impact which should be felt by the reader. The writer should write keeping in view the skill, knowledge, status and understanding ability of the reader. The correct use of words and phrases establishes a proper relationship and link to make the intended messages clear.

3) Relevant information : It should provide relevant information and details which go into forming various part of the message. It is complete when it contains all relevant facts and details which the receiver needs to know.

4) Brevity : It means that the message should be brief and yet convey effectively the intended meaning using minimum words, is indeed a very fine art in communication. The receiver does not have unlimited time to spare towards reading a letter. It should be written in such a manner that a proper attention is caught by the reader.

5) Simplicity : It refers to the ease of understanding. A simple understandable writing catches attention more quickly and makes the desired impact. Keep it short and simple should be the motto of letter writing.

6) Timeliness : Letter should be written and dispatched in time. This is specially required when the letter carries any urgent message.

7) Language : The language used in a business letter should be easy and appropriate. Special attention should be given to the phrases, expressions, words, grammar and spellings as it carries a lot of impression of the organization.

8) Vocabulary or Word Power : Words are the very essence of written communication. Words translate thoughts and carry the message through to the reader. Most of the words or set of words depend on the context, tone and gravity of the message and also the relationship with the person to whom it is addressed.

9) Appeal : A letter should be formulated in such a manner that it conveys an overall impression through elegance, taste, beauty and decency. The writer should put himself in the reader's shoe and think according to the readers view. A good letter makes the reader feel important. Overwriting, correction, unintended gaps steal the elegance of a good letter.

10) Style : It refers to the presentation skill and the manner of writing. A simple, informal, considerate and focused style scores high in the mind of the reader. Good writing style is an indication to a sincere effort. It should also have politeness or courtesy and respect the reader as an individual.

11) Striving for excellence : A good writer should always try to achieve high standard of writing skill to reach the level of excellence. The bigger the letter, the more complex

it becomes and greater the scope for skillful writing.

TYPES OF LETTERS :

Business letters – There are many ways of classifying business letter.

1) Information letters : Types of these letters are :

a) Routine letters – enquiries, quotations, orders, payment letters.

b) Special purpose letters

2) Sales letters – Offers, etc.

3) Problem letters – Complaints, overdue accounts, etc.

4) Goodwill letters – Greetings, Thank you letters.

Sometimes all letters cannot be easily included in the above classification. Letters can also be classified on the basis of our approach.

1) Direct letters – all letters related to offers of appointment, enquiries, orders, promotion, intimation are categorized in this category.

2) Indirect letters : all letters related to refusals and rejections fall in this category.

3) Persuasive : Offers of sales and services, job applications and sales proposal letters fall under this category.

Letters can also be classified as :

a) Official letters : Letters written to government officials or semi government departments or offices.

b) D.O. (Demi Official letters) : They are essentially official in purpose but addressed to an official by name. A demi official letter is sent to guard the confidential nature of the matter concerned. They also invite personal attention of the addressee.

c) Form letters : They are used for correspondence of routine nature. Acknowledgement, reminders, interviews, notices, appointments, etc, fall in the category of form letters.

d) Internal letters : Also referred to as Memo, which are generally used in business organizations for internal communications.

PARTS OF A BUSINESS LETTER :

A letter can be divided into the following parts :

a) Heading : This contains the name of the company or firm in which the sender belongs.

b) Reference No : An unique number that is put on every letter for future reference.

c) Date : On the top right hand corner in the format Month Date, Year.

d) Inside Address : This is written below the reference number which contains the name and address and to whom the letter is sent.

e) Attention line : Kind Attention Mr. ....., in this format is given below the address.

f) Subject line : This is mentioned after the Kind Attention line which gives a brief of the subject of the letter.

g) Salutation : It begins from the left hand margin to address the person to whom the letter is sent and is followed by a comma, eg, Dear Sir / Madam,

h) Body : It is the main part of information of a letter. It should start below the salutation with a line space from the left hand margin.

i) Signature : The signature is placed just below the complimentary close. The name of the signatory is typed in bracket below the space left for the signature. The designation is written below the name, eg, Yours truly,
(Dr A Pandey)
Professor, Author.

j) Complimentary close : Written two lines below the last line of the text of the letter. It is placed on the left hand margin and is followed by a comma. It should be remembered that 'Yours' is used when the name is used in the salutation. 'Respectfully' is used only when writing to high public officials.

k) Reference section : Enclosures or courtesy copies (cc : also referred to as carbon copies)is mentioned here.

l) Post script : Optional bit of writing at the end which is mainly a friendly and informal note which is not related to the main part of the letter.

BUSINESS LETTER FORMAT :

Name of the Sender's Organisation

Ref No : .... Date : ....

To (Name to the person to whome the letter is addressed)

....

....

Kind Attention : (Name of the Concerned person)

Subject : ________________________(Jest of the Letter)

Dear Sir/Madam,

This is to ....

....

....

....

....

....

Yours truly,

(Dr A Pandey)

Professor, Author.

NINE

BARRIERS OF COMMUNICATION

BARRIERS OF COMMUNICATION:

Communication is not always successful. Certain barriers affect the clarity, accuracy and effectiveness of the message. There may be some fault in the communication process which may prevent the message from reaching.

Categorization of barriers :

a) **Semantic barriers** : Different people assign different meanings to one specific message which may be due to the problem with meaning, significance or content. These are barriers due to the literal meanings of the words or phrases used in the communication process.

Few examples of semantic barriers are :

1) Words that have similar pronunciation but multiple meaning.
2) Badly expressed message.
3) Wrong interpretation
4) Unqualified assumptions
5) Technical language

b) **Organizational barrier** : This problem is due to the physical distance between members with respect to their functional specialization of tasks, authority, status, etc.

Few categories of organizational barriers are :

1) Organizational culture and climate
2) Organizational rules and regulations
3) Status relationship – not being able to speak because of lack of authority
4) Complexity in organizational structure – may be too mu7ch divisionalisation may not facilitate a free flow of communication
5) Lack of co-operation between superiors and subordinates.

c) **Interpersonal barrier** : Barriers in communication which are based and developed on relationships, values held and attitudes of the participant in the process of communication. It is highly noticed in a superior – subordinate relationship.

Reasons of interpersonal barriers from superiors are :

1) Shortage of time for employees
2) Lack of trust
3) Lack of consideration for employee needs
4) Wish to capture authority
5) Fear of losing power of control
6) Bypassing
7) Information overload

Reasons of interpersonal barriers from subordinates are :

1) Lack of proper channel
2) No interest to communicate
3) Lack of co-operation
4) Lack of trust
5) Poor relationship between superior and sunbordinate

6) Fear of penalty.

d) **Individual Barriers** : They are called psycho-sociological barriers which arises due to differences in individual competencies to think and act. It is also because of individual skills in receiving and transmitting information which includes poor listening and improper reading skills.

Individual barriers occur due to :

1) Style – linguistic accent, form of expression by idioms or phrases, type of humour, etc.
2) Selective perception – orthodox thinking which is previously decided earlier.
3) Halo effect – guided by unchangeable thoughts.
4) Status relationship – Superiority or inferiority complex.
5) Poor attention and retention – nature of an individual different from others.
6) Inattention – busy with other jobs rather paying attention.
7) Undue importance of written words – going by the words and not the meaning.
8) Defensiveness – trying to protect oneself and having prior judgement.
9) Closed mind – thoughtlessness.
10) State of health – sick personnel.
11) Filtering – using own idea into the meaning and modifying.

e) **Cross cultural barriers** : These are referred to as geographic barriers which are due to the difference in time or geographic location. There may also be communication barriers due to cultural and social factors prevalent in different countries. Words, colour and symbols have different meaning in different cultures.

f) **Physical barriers** / channels and media barriers : The accuracy of communication that is affected by physical barriers like distance, noise or even the disturbance of the medium used in the communication process.

They are characterized by :

1) Noise – which can cause disturbance in the hearing
2) Environment – not very suitable for the communication.
3) Circumstantial factors – barriers due to situation crisis
4) Defects in the media - Media not responding in terms of proper reception.

g) **Technological barriers** : Barriers that arise due to technological advancements in the field of communication are termed under this heading. Technology generates lots of information which is beyond the capacity of the recipient. Technological advancements increases barriers and so every individual must try to keep updated as much as possible.

MEASURES TO OVERCOME BARRIERS IN COMMUNICATION

There are numerous ways by which barriers can be overcome so that communication is effective.

1) Fostering good relationship.
2) Purposeful and well focused communication
3) Good co-ordination between superior and subordinate
4) Avoid technical language
5) Feedback
6) Accuracy
7) Clarity
8) Communication of organizational philosophy.
9) Organisational structure
10) Division of labour.
11) Organisational policies.
12) Minimize semantic problems

13) Proper communication channels.
14) Right feedback.

Constant effort is required to overcome barriers which unconsciously creep up in the process of communication. A constant check during the process is required for overcoming any possible barrier. Both the sender and the receiver has to work together for an effective communication.

TEN

COMMUNICATION TIPS FOR THE SMART KID ON THE BLOCK

- **Give Your Whole Attention**

Have you ever been in communication where someone was busy looking at their smartphone while talking or listening to you? That's called being absent-minded. It's a sign of poor communication. Therefore, be mindful of how you're communicating. Offering a full focus by maintaining eye contact during conversations and meetings will contribute greatly to effective communication. Nod your head affirmatively while in a conversation to convey your focus visually.

- **Get a Team Communication App**

Lack of communication can be a major buzzkill for numerous workplace failures. Team communication apps are getting quite popular today to make life easier and collaborate well. It is actually quite time-consuming for teams, clients, and managers to keep track of long email threads. This is where the team collaboration app makes all the difference – helps users to work together on different activities and projects and breaks all barriers to effective communication.

Every project needs an effective communication stream to reflect the progress of the project. The modern workplace is on its way to digital transformation. So, you need to invest in key systems and applications for productivity and communication. According to the needs of your project, communication tools can be an effective way for the whole team to meet up. With task management software, you can make communication streamlined between your team members. They can exchange messages about the tasks and all relevant information can be shared in the same place. It prevents long email threads that have long been one of the communication approaches. With an understanding, the technology is evolving to support you always.

- **Inform and Inspire**

More than just passing on the information, be careful of explaining and clarifying your thoughts and ideas to have an effective one. Passing the information is just half the equation. Plan ahead what you want the audience to remember from the conversation. Do you want them to take any kind of action? The most effective communication will make your people take action.

- **Practice Active Listening**

Employees who listen well tend to work better. Listening is twice as important as talking and one big important part of effective communication skills in business. Listening should not be taken for granted. Do not just sit back, barely awake, letting the speaker's words wash over you. The more you listen well, the better you receive the information.

Do you know how to listen well? Here's how?

Make eye contact with the speaker

Respond appropriately

No interruptions, please

Examine your body language

Choose the Best Method of communication

To communicate well means to understand and be understood. Knowing the right methods of communication is as important as having effective communication skills.

Visual communication via charts, maps, images, and graphs.

Verbal communication through face to face, by phone, and other media.

Non-verbal communication through body language, eye contact, gestures.

Written communication through letters, e-mails, books, magazines, and the internet.

- **Don't Beat Around the Bush**

Keeping in mind the importance of communication at the workplace, the next big thing is clear, concise communication. Whether you're into verbal communication or non-verbal communication, do not get into a long speech to get your point across. You do want to respect everyone's time, so be brief, to the point, and balance brevity with a human touch.

- **Personal Skills**

Interpersonal communication skills will do good for both your professional and personal life. You will need it every day in your life. It includes skills related to emotional intelligence or being able to understand your own and others' emotions. For example, high self-esteem and confidence can help you have more positivity about yourself and what you can do, including communication. And positivity leads to effectiveness.

- **Confident, Persuasive, and Patient**

There is a difference between being able to communicate and communicating effectively. Along with the above tips, having just a little patience, confidence and persuasiveness can help you communicate your information more effectively. Confidence means taking care of what your body language is. Your own sense of self-worth will make you feel effective, rather than helpless.

- **Smile**

Keep your arms uncrossed
Maintain an erect posture
Maintain eye contact
Keep your devices away
Use time wisely

Utilizing coffee breaks can keep the team-building spirit strong and give everyone an opportunity to get to know each other better. Team bonding is a better way to improve communication channels. Coffee breaks is an ideal opportunity for informal meetings and discussions. It encourages healthy communication amongst colleagues and also promotes the exchange of ideas. Let your team members have coffee breaks at the same time to create an ideal environment for team members to relax and discuss issues. And this art of conversation will often encourage the team to discuss work as well. Thus coffee will not only act as an energy booster throughout the day but also promote productivity with relaxed conversations.

- **Conduct team-building activities**

Team building activities have a great impact on the productivity and overall teamwork of your team. It can help your people to communicate better, and also help them to build good relationships with one another. Create structure opportunities for your employees to collaborate through activities like team lunch, ice breaker games in meetings, group meetings, fitness sessions, puzzle-solving games, or any outdoor activity. You can schedule these activities at the end of the month or weekly to get your team together in the room.

- **Show appreciation**

Tell your employees, coworkers, and colleagues about how much you care and respect them. Showing appreciation is an effective way to deal with low employee morale and to make your team members feel like they matter. This is a method to promote communication in the team. Give a token of appreciation to your team members by congratulating them for great ideas, thanking a team member for finishing a task, and expressing gratitude even for small acts.

- **Encourage two-way feedback**

In order to have a smooth work environment, it is important to have two-way communication. In the workplace, feedback is important to generate results, where the main objective is to strengthen progress towards company goals. A common mistake that leaders make when offering feedback is turning it into one way dialogue (feedback). They give no opportunity to employees to present their own comments and concerns. Encouraging two-way feedback is a sign of good communication in the workplace that will give your team a chance to self-evaluate. Give detailed feedback to increase team communication and to coach your team members. You can keep a written record of feedback via your task management system which can help increase overall communication and productivity.

- **Having One-on-One Interactions**

Successful teams are made of team members who are purposeful in their interactions. One-on-one interactions are important with every individual you hire to make sure employee engagement doesn't fall short in your workplace. During these interactions, set your expectations and needs. Tell them about what your project demands, what are the norms of your company for employees, and give them adequate preparation time to maximize their potential. When having one-on-one interactions, make sure you know when to listen to what your employees have to say. The leaders need to put their best foot forward for their new hires to get to the bottom of things.

- **Effective Communication Skills**

Growing better communication habits for the future means practicing effective communication skills and being a powerful communicator. But what are the examples of effective communication? Well, here are 3 communication skills you should work on:

Be aware of your body

Your body tells a story about you.

Crossed or folded arms – Defensiveness

Hands held behind the body – Confidence

Mending clothes, accessories, watch– Nervousness

Clenched fists – Anger or anxiety

Squeezing hands – Self-soothing

Active listening – That means being completely present of what the speaker is trying to impart.

Delivering with confidence – You need to develop a strong delivery by being patient, kind to yourself, and slowing down.

Keep it Positive- Last but not least, try to stay positive. No matter whatever state of mind you are in, being positive will save you from getting into a bad conversation.

Author

Dr Anshumali Pandey, Author.

Dr. Anshumali Pandey, is a renowned & reliable name in the field of Education, Hospitality, Tourism and Tribal Food. He is a Teacher and Chef by profession, and also an Author, a Business Auditor, and an avid culinary traveller to the Indian Sub continental hinterlands. Dr. Anshumali Pandey is a Hospitality Educator (PhD) who specialises in Higher Education, Office Administration, Pay roll, HR, Labour Laws, Audit, and Procurement & Tender Process. He is an Author with 39 Publications consisting of 24 Books.

The books written by Dr Anshumali Pandey are essentially a banquet arising from an experience of over 25 years of Professional life and have boiled down to crisp and accurate writing on his favourite subjects. Hospitality Sector champion requires to be a specialist in many fields and Dr Pandey is one of them. His knowledge is evident from the spectrum of subjects which he has chosen for his books so far, which ranges from being a specialist chef, to Master of Human resources, to Education and to love for children, and topped with Spirituality.

Books written by the Author are –

1. Theory of Indian Cookery
2. Beauty and Irony of Silvassa Tourism
3. A Short Indian Food Story
4. Be Your Own Guide to Indian Cuisine
5. Cookery Fundamentals
6. History of Indian Food
7. The Great Indian Story Book for Children
8. Personal Budget: Easy Work Book
9. Online Classes Log Book
10. Dictionary Making Work Book for School Children
11. The Lazy Bed
12. Hindu Dharm (In Hindi Language)
13. Where is my coffee?
14. Your First Job is Never your Last (Volume 1)
15. You are Almost There (Quick Fix Resume and Interview Hacks)
16. Working for the Enemy? - A lesson in Career Management
17. Public Speaking for the Young
18. A Date With Coffee
19. How to be The Best Hotel Front Office Employee
20. Diploma in Food Production, The complete Syllabus
21. Diploma in F&B Service, The Complete Syllabus
22. Diploma in Front Office, The Complete Syllabus

23. The Time to Speak is Now
24. Munshi Premchand (Short Stories in English)

Connect with me: anshumali.pandey@gmail.com
https://notionpress.com/author/337004

For further details please scan the QR code.

9 798885 917254